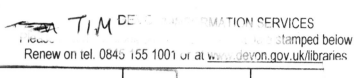

WATERLOO WEST

ROGER SIVITER ARPS

Front cover: On Saturday 11 October 1986, Class 33 Type 3 diesel No 33040 hurries towards Buckhorn Weston tunnel, two miles west of Gillingham (Dorset) with the Saturdays-only 09.13 from Brighton to Exeter. *Roger Siviter*

Back cover: The end of the summer timetable in 1987 (3 October) saw the end of the locomotive-hauled trains on the Exeter to Barnstaple branch. On the penultimate Saturday of the summer timetable, 26 September, Class 33 No 33023, having just arrived with the 12.18 from Exeter St Davids, is seen running round its train prior to leaving on the 13.53 return working for Exeter. Note the Barnstaple Junction sign, a reminder of the time when the station was the junction for the popular north Devon seaside resort of Ilfracombe.
Christina Siviter

Right: Red-liveried Class 47 No 47703 leaves Salisbury behind as it heads into the setting sun with the 16.55 Waterloo to Exeter train on 8 August 1991. In the background is Salisbury's medieval cathedral. *Roger Siviter*

© Roger Siviter 2002
Published by Great Bear Publishing
4 Shannon Way, Evesham WR11 3FF Tel: 01386 765134

ISBN 0-9541150-1-5

Designed and produced by Viners Wood Associates Tel: 01452 812813
Printed in England by Ian Allan Ltd, Surrey.

Above: A classic scene at Waterloo, taken from the block of flats just to the west of the station on 9 February 1989, as Class 33 No 33115 propels the 13.59 ex Basingstoke into the former LSWR/SR terminus. This station was opened around 1840, with lines to Basingstoke and Southampton. Exeter was reached by the LSWR in 1860. On the left hand side can be seen Class 50 No 50036 *Victorious* waiting to leave on the 15.10 to Exeter.

Hugh Ballantyne

Opposite: Night and day at Waterloo. In the top picture, Class 47/7 No 4770 heads the 17.05 to Exeter on 14 January 1993. Whilst below, Class 50 No 5004 *Dauntless* has just arrived at platform 13 with the 06.45 train from Exeter.

Top: *Geoff Gillham* Bottom: *Roger Sivite*

Introduction

Since the LSWR line to Exeter and the south-west was completed in the latter half of the 19th century, many changes have taken place. The route of the Atlantic Coast Express (ACE) and the line to Plymouth via Oakhampton was truncated, leaving only the section from Exeter to Meldon Quarry on the Plymouth line and the line to Barnstaple, originally the junction for Ilfracombe to the north and Halwill Junction (for Bude) to the south. These closures took place from the late 1960s until 1982, when the Barnstaple to Torrington section, which had been kept open for goods traffic, was closed.

Steam power on the Waterloo-Exeter line had more or less ended by 1965 with the closure to steam of Exmouth Junction shed in that year, and diesel traction – mainly in the form of the Type 4 Warship Class diesels – now held sway. These locomotives were in charge until their withdrawal in 1971 (when most of the Class were withdrawn) by which time the Sultzer Type 3 locomotives (Class 33s), popularly known as 'Cromptons' because of their Crompton Parkinson nose-suspended traction motors, became the main motive power until the advent of the more powerful English Electric Class 50 locomotives in 1980. The Class 50s, together with the Class 47s and the Class 33s, were in charge of the passenger trains until 1992/1993 when the turbo units appeared and ended many years of locomotive-hauled travel on this famous route.

This book is a journey from Waterloo to Barnstaple from the mid-1960s to the early 1990s when the locomotive-hauled train reigned supreme.

In compiling this book I should like to thank the following people: Hugh Ballantyne, Tom Heavyside, Bryan Hicks, Geoff Gillham, my wife Christina and – most important of all – the railwaymen who made it all possible.

Roger Siviter
Evesham, July 2002

BIBLIOGRAPHY

British Railways Past add Present No 8 Devon
David Mitchell (Silver Link Publishing, Ltd.)

British Railways Past and Present No 22 Wiltshire
Graham Roose and Hugh Ballantyne (Silver Link Publishing, Ltd)

British Railways Past and Present No 29 Dorset
Terry Gough and David Mitchell (Silver Link Publishing, Ltd.)

50s to Exeter
Roger Siviter (Silver Link Publishing, Ltd.)

Also available in the Great Bear 'Yesteryear Traction' series:
50s West – Exeter to Penzance, Roger Siviter. Price £14.99

With 'Big Ben' and the Houses of Parliament in the background, immaculate Crompton No 33118 races through Vauxhall with the 10.10 Waterloo to Salisbury train on 21 July 1983. This train is scheduled to take 103 minutes for the 83¾ mile journey, which includes six stops.

Hugh Ballantyne

Brush Type 5 Class 56 diesel No 56110 makes leisurely progress through one of the busiest railway junctions in the world – Clapham – with a westbound freight on 27 April 1991. These powerful Class 56 diesels were first introduced in 1976, No 56110 having been built by British Rail Engineering, Ltd. (BREL). Sadly, the over-line signal box has now been demolished.

Roger Siviter

After Clapham Junction, the LSWR line to Basingstoke and Salisbury leaves behind the lines to Reading, Gatwick Airport and the south east suburban lines to Oxted, and heads west through the outer London suburbs, passing through commuter towns such as Walton on Thames (17 miles from Waterloo) where on the 21 August 1991 we see Class 50 No 50002 *Superb* at high speed with the 15.15 Waterloo to Exeter train.

Hugh Ballantyne

Weybridge station, some two miles west of Walton on Thames, is situated at the end of a deep cutting which runs for a mile and a half east of the station. On Saturday 27 April 1991, No 33102 leaves the cutting behind as it hurries through Weybridge station on the down fast line with the 17.15 Waterloo to Exeter train. Earlier in the day it had worked into Waterloo with the 10.20 from Exeter.

Roger Siviter

Still clean after a recent repaint and carrying its original number (6532) Class 33 No 33114 powers the 10.00 Waterloo to Salisbury away from Woking on 22 January 1992. Note the wooden platform canopies and the Southern Railway 'modern' concrete signal box.

Geoff Gillham

Our next picture was taken some five miles west of Woking at Deep Cut which is just to the west of Pirbright Junction (for the Aldershot branch). This location on the Surrey/Hampshire border, with its four-track section and gentle curves, has always been a popular spot with railway photographers – I well remember photographing steam in this area in 1966. On 11 April 1991, No 33103 in the 'Dutch' livery is caught by the camera as it heads west with an empty ballast train, probably bound for Exeter and Meldon Quarry.

Roger Siviter

Looking smart in its Network SouthEast livery, Class 47/7 No 47709 speeds through Winchfield station on 26 July 1991 with the 10.00 Waterloo to Exeter train. Note the two distinct styles of platform canopies. These veteran Brush Type 4 diesel locomotives were first introduced in 1962 and with variou modifications, etc. have been in main line service for 40 years, and are onl now, in 2002/3, finishing their days.

Roger Sivite

On 15 October 1966, Class 42 Warship hydraulic diesel No D824 *Highflyer* is photographed near Hook, two miles west of Winchfield, with a midday Exeter to Waterloo train, composed mainly of Southern stock. The Type 4 Warships were introduced in 1958 and worked on the Waterloo to Exeter route between 1964 and 1971, the year before they were all finally withdrawn from service. No 824 was amongst the last batch to be withdrawn in December 1972. Happily, several examples remain in preservation.

Bryan Hicks

Opposite: Class 47/7 No 47708 *Waverley* leaves Basingstoke station with the 06.19 Exeter to Waterloo train on 22 April 1993, a few weeks prior to the end of scheduled locomotive haulage on the route. This ended on Saturday 10 July 1993 without ceremony. This picture well illustrates Basingstoke's four through platforms, still with SR-style canopies. It is also the junction station for the line to Reading, which runs (out of sight) behind the train and the modern-looking signal box.

Hugh Ballantyne

Above: Two miles west of Basingstoke is Worting junction, where the Exeter and Southampton/Bournemouth lines diverge via the Battledown flyover. On the morning of 12 August 1991 Class 47/7 No 47703 *The Queen Mother*, in Parcels Sector Red livery, threads the famous junction and heads for Basingstoke and Waterloo with the 08.10 Exeter to Waterloo train. Worthy of note is the elderly-looking plate-layer's hut of galvanised metal construction. Also, at the rear of the train can be seen the flyover which carries the up Southampton and Bournemouth line, the down line for Southampton being the left hand line, with the two centre lines being the up and down Exeter route.

Roger Siviter

This view taken on 20 April 1991 shows clearly the Battledown flyover, which was constructed in 1897. The train is the 06.45 Exeter to Waterloo, hauled by English Electric Class 50 No 50017 *Royal Oak*, resplendent in Network SouthEast livery.

Roger Siviter

As a complete contrast to locomotive-hauled travel, we see a Class 207 East Sussex three-car DEMU No 207005 as it pulls out of the attractive former LSWR station at Whitchurch (Hants) with the 09.40 Salisbury to Basingstoke stopping train. These non-gangwayed units were built at the Southern Region Eastleigh works in 1962.

Roger Siviter

On 12 August 1991, Class 47/7 No 47707 *Holyrood* crosses over Hurstbourne viaduct with the 13.15 Waterloo to Exeter train. This attractive eight-arch viaduct, one of the few on the line, is situated two miles to the west of Whitchurch and crosses over the River Bourne. This area of Hampshire is also famous for its watercress beds.

Roger Sivite

Our next location is Andover, junction for the freight-only line to Ludgershall, once part of the through route to Savernake. On 25 August 1981, unrebuilt Class 50 No 50044 *Exeter* pulls out of the busy-looking Andover station and heads for Salisbury with the 11.10 Waterloo to Exeter train. These powerful 2700hp locomotives first appeared regularly on the route in 1980, which led to an acceleration of the train times. From the late 1970s to the early 1980s, the class were all refurbished with most of them being turned out in the BR 'large logo' livery and also named. Many of the class have been preserved, including No 50044.

Tom Heavyside

Above: A pair of 'Cromptons' – Nos 33031 and 33033 – provide super power for the lightweight 10.10 Waterloo to Salisbury service, seen here at Monxton, just west of Andover, on 30 June 1988. *Hugh Ballantyne*

Opposite: Today, Grateley station has been completely refurbished, but when this picture was taken of Class 42 Warship No D811 *Daring* heading west through Grateley on 10 June 1967 with a Waterloo to Exeter train, it was looking very run down. Refurbishment took place in the 1980s, with the revival of the

route, caused mainly by the acceleration of the journey times. As can be seen Grateley at one time had many sidings, probably for military traffic from the branch line to Bulford Camp – this branch line was also connected to Amesbury Junction (for Salisbury) as well as Grateley. Passenger traffic on the Bulford branch ceased on 30 June 1952, but goods traffic lasted until 4 March 1963. I well remember this branch line, being stationed there during my army service in 1954/5, and travelling on a troop train in January 1955 from Bulford Camp to Harwich. *Bryan Hick*

Left: Shortly after leaving Grateley (73 miles fro Waterloo) we enter the county of Wiltshire and t county town of Salisbury. On 30 August 199 Class 50 No 50005 *Collingwood* leaves Fishert tunnel and threads Salisbury Tunnel junction w the 10.20 Exeter to Waterloo train. The line on t left is to Southampton and Eastleigh. *Roger Sivit*

Opposite: Passing a fine display of flowerin broom, grey liveried Class 37 No 37072 heac downgrade out of Fisherton tunnel towarc Salisbury station with the 10.34 Fawley t Tavistock junction fuel oil tanks on Monday 18 Ma 1992. Above the train is the A36 trunk road whic at this point forms part of a ring road round th ancient capital of Wiltshire. *Geoff Gillhar*

Left: Class 50 No 50037 *Illustrious* climbs out of Salisbury and heads for Waterloo on the late afternoon of 8 August 1991 with the 16.22 train from Exeter. To complete the scene is Salisbury cathedral with its 400 feet high spire, the highest medieval spire in Europe. *Roger Siviter*

Above: This view of Salisbury station, looking east, was taken on a wet but photogenic Sunday 7 April 1991, and shows well the curving platforms and wooden canopies, and also the attractive ironwork supports and posts. On the left is a Class 205 Hampshire three-car unit No 205028 waiting to leave on the 15.25 stopping train to Basingstoke, whilst stabled on the right hand side are Class 50 No 50017 *Royal Oak* and Class 33 No 33102. I have many memories of Salisbury station in my army days. One that stands out is arriving at the station with many other squaddies around 2.30 in the morning (a gang of us would often catch a late evening train from Birmingham Snow Hill) to return to Bulford Camp, and knowing that there was just one taxi available (usually an Austin Big 6) – you can imagine the rush to get out of the station. Oh the joys of National Service! *Roger Siviter*

In grey and yellow livery, English Electric Class 73/1 Electro-Diesel locomotive No 73129 *City of Winchester* pulls through Salisbury on 8 August 1991 with a nuclear flask train bound for Westbury. On the left hand side is the old LSWR signal box, now used as a store.

Roger Siviter

During the autumn of 1991, Class 37s made several appearances on the Waterloo-Exeter route as substitute power. On the evening of Sunday 29 September 1991, No 37098 has replaced defective Class 47 No 47717 at Salisbury and waits to head west with the 18.55 from Waterloo. *Geoff Gillham*

Above: Salisbury in 'semaphore' days, as Class 33 No 33009 runs into the station on 10 September 1977 with the 11.00 Exeter to Waterloo train. The line on the left hand side also led to Salisbury shed (72B) which was situated on the south side of the line, about half a mile west of the station. This shed, which closed in 1967 with the end of Southern Region steam working, had a high reputation for the turn-out of its locomotives. I know from a visit I made to the depot on Maunday Thursday, 2 April 1966, that most of the engines were in very good external condition. *Hugh Ballantyne*

Opposite: On a misty autumn day in 1986 (2 October) Class 33 No 33062 climbs out of Salisbury with the 08.10 Portsmouth to Cardiff train, which will leave the LSWR Exeter route in about a mile at Wilton junction. Originally, the GWR line to Westbury ran parallel but unconnected to the SR route from Salisbury station until they divided at Wilton. Note the railway allotment, a reminder of 'war-time' days. *Roger Siviter*

Left: I mentioned before that there are few viaducts on this route. One of these is the small but pleasant three-arch viaduct at Barford St. Martin, some five miles west of Salisbury. On the evening of Wednesday 28 August 1991, the last 'large logo' liveried Class 50 No 50046 *Ajax* crosses the viaduct and heads west with the 16.15 from Waterloo to Yeovil Junction train. This will be returning at 19.00 as an ECS train to Eastleigh.

Roger Siviter

Opposite: After Wilton junction, the line was singled to Templecombe with the exception of passing loops and also the up line from Dinton to a nearby military depot. On 29 August 1970 Brush Type 4 No D1595 (47469) is seen on that up line approaching Chilmark siding box (disused) with an explosives train from Glascoed, in South Wales, to RAF Chilmark.

Hugh Ballantyne

Apart from the appearance of the powerful Class 50s on the route in 1980, another factor for the improvement in times was the provision of a loop at Tisbury (some 12 miles west of Salisbury) which could accommodate a 12-coach train. Heading west out of Tisbury loop on 18 April 1989, after waiting to cross an up train, is Class 33/1 No 33102 and 4TC set 8001 forming the 12.1? from Waterloo to Gillingham (Dorset). No 33102 was one of a number of th? class fitted for push-pull working. Part of the small town of Tisbury can b? glimpsed on the left hand side behind the oak tree.

Geoff Gillhar?

30

'Large logo' liveried Class 50 No 50012 *Benbow* approaches Tisbury on 2 October 1986 with the 09.38 Exeter to Waterloo service. With an arrival at Waterloo at 13.02, this train was allowed 204 minutes for the 172½ mile journey, which included 14 stops.

Roger Siviter

After Tisbury, the line runs through the beautiful rolling Wiltshire countryside.
Class 47/7 No 47708, still in distinctive ScotRail livery, leaves Tisbury behind
and heads west with the 08.40 Waterloo to Exeter train, on 13 August 1991.

Roger Siviter

On the same day a few minutes later and now looking westwards, we see No 7702 *Saint Cuthbert*, a former ScotRail locomotive but now in Network outhEast livery, heading past Tisbury Gates with the 08.10 from Exeter to Waterloo. At one time, these gates were manually operated, but now have electronically controlled barriers. Note the SR signal box behind the train.

Roger Siviter

An interesting scene, photographed just east of Semley on 10 April 1991, is the annual weed-killing train hauled by two English Electric Type 1 diesels with No 20901 leading and No 20904 bringing up the rear as they head for Salisbury.

These 1000 horse power locomotives were first introduced in 1957 and we built over the next 11 years. Now in private ownership for the weed-killing tra their original numbers were 20041 and 20101.

Roger Sivi

We now leave Wiltshire and cross into Dorset where, at Gillingham on the morning of 29 August 1970, Class 42 Warship hydraulic diesel No D827 *Kelly* pulls out of the station with the 08.50 Exeter to Waterloo train. *Kelly* was built at BR Swindon in 1960 and withdrawn in January 1972.

Hugh Ballantyne

It is 7.48am on the morning of 29 August 1991, as Class 47/7 No 47710 arrives at the newly painted Gillingham station with the first Exeter to Waterloo train of the day, which departed from Exeter St Davids station at 06.11. Note the handsome LSWR station building with its steeply pitched roof and, at the end of the down platform, the functional looking signal box, which was built in 195[...]. The large fertilizer store now occupies the land where the small goods she[...] and yard used to be.

Roger Sivi[...]

Departing from Gillingham 21 years to the day before the previous picture are two Type 3 'Cromptons', Nos D6566 (33048) and D6588 (33203) on the 08.50 Brighton to Exeter train. Note the first locomotive is in the old green livery, and the second engine is in what was then the new blue livery. *Hugh Ballantyne*

Above: On the afternoon of 29 August 1991, Class 50 No 50033 *Glorious* climbs the 1 in 100 towards Buckhorn Weston (or Gillingham) tunnel with the 13.15 Waterloo to Exeter train. *Roger Siviter*

Opposite: Turning round from the previous picture, and on the same day, we see Class 47/7 No 47703 *The Queen Mother* in Parcels Sector Red livery leaving Buckhorn Weston tunnel and heading for Gillingham and Waterloo with the 08.10 train from Exeter. The tunnel mouth can be seen at the rear of the train. *Roger Siviter*

The next stop after Gillingham is Templecombe, famous for being the junction station which connected the Waterloo-Exeter line with the Somerset & Dorset Joint Railway (SDJR) which ran from Bath to Bournemouth, Sadly, this line closed in March 1966. Templecombe (SR) also closed in May 1966 but was reopened in 1982 and, with help from the local community rail action group, a new station building was completed by 1988. Entering the 'new' station ⊙ 29 July 1991 is Class 47/7 No 47716 with the 08.10 Exeter to Waterloo train. the end of the platform is the former SR signal box which now also serves as ticket office, and on the right hand side edge is a sign denoting th Templecombe is 'Britain's Best Kept Small Station'.

Roger Sivit

Sunday 24 May 1992 saw the end of regular Class 50 workings on the route. To commemorate this, several trains were double-headed by 'celebrity' locomotives of that famous Class, namely D400 (formerly 50050 *Fearless*) and 50007 *Sir Edward Elgar*. The immaculate pair of 'Hoovers' are seen here near Stowell, providing super power for the 09.28 Exeter-Waterloo train. *Roger Siviter*

Opposite: Class 47/7 No 47716 approaches the summit of Sherborne bank near Milborne Port with the 11.50 Exeter to Waterloo train on Saturday 27 July 1991.
Roger Siviter

Above: On the same day as the previous picture, Class 50 No 50030 *Repulse* heads down Sherborne bank with the 15.15 Waterloo to Exeter train. This bank is around 4 miles long, from Sherborne up to Milborne Port, and with a gradient as steep as 1 in 80 it would have meant hard work in 'steam days' for the footplate men.
Roger Siviter

On 15 August 1991, Class 33 No 33102 runs through the beautiful Dorset countryside near Sherborne with the 15.15 Waterloo to Exeter service. The following day, red-liveried Class 47/7 No 47712 *Lady Diana Spencer* starts the climb out of the ancient market town of Sherborne with the 17.38 train from Exeter to Waterloo. The remains of Sherborne Old Castle complete this idyllically rural scene.

Both pictures: *Roger Siviter*

After Sherborne, we reach the important junction station at Yeovil, some 123 miles from Waterloo. Yeovil Junction, which is situated about a mile south of the town just on the Dorset/Somerset border, is the junction for Yeovil Pen Mill station on the former GWR line from Westbury to Weymouth. This line runs under the Waterloo-Exeter line just east of Yeovil Junction. A busy scene at Yeovil Junction station on the evening of 15 April 1993 as Class 47/7 No 47711

County of Hertfordshire approaches the station with the 15.15 Waterloo to Exeter service to be greeted by No 47702 *Saint Cuthbert* waiting to leave on the 16.22 Exeter to Waterloo train. On the left hand side is the LSWR signal box and also the junction line to Yeovil Pen Mill, and in the foreground are the lines leading back to the small coal depot.

Roger Sivite

On 10 October 1990, English Electric Class 37 No 37212, having run round on arrival at Yeovil Junction, is seen in the up road with the Wednesdays-only Speedlink coal train from Radyr, South Wales. Having discharged its load in the adjacent coal siding, the train will return to South Wales via Castle Cary and Westbury. Note that only platforms one and two are now in public use, hence the truncated footbridge.

Hugh Ballantyne

With plenty of 'clag', Class 47/7 No 47708 makes a spirited departure out of Yeovil Junction station on Sunday 21 June 1992 with the 10.40 Waterloo to Exeter train. Dominating the foreground is the locomotive turntable which, together with the adjacent buildings, forms part of the Yeovil Railway Centre.

Roger Siviter

Class 50 No 50018 *Resolution* leaves Yeovil Junction with the 17.05 Waterloo to Exeter train on 30 August 1990. These popular English Electric locomotives were first introduced in 1967, from which time until their transfer to the Western Region in 1976 they worked mainly on the West Coast route between Crewe and Glasgow. By 1992 they had all been withdrawn from service, No 50018 being withdrawn in July 1991. Many examples of this class have been preserved and some work main line specials.

Roger Siviter

Left: Class 47/7 No 47710 and its rake of Network SouthEast liveried coaches make a fine sight as they speed westwards through the lovely Somerset countryside near Coker Wood, some 4 miles to the west of Yeovil Junction. The train is the 11.00 Waterloo to Exeter and the date is 29 August 1991. *Roger Sivite*

Opposite: Just east of the market town of Crewkerne are the small villages of North and South Perrott, which are divided by the Waterloo-Exeter line. On Sunday 24 May 1992, two Class 33s, Nos 33002 and 33102, head eastward through this attractive location with the 14.2? Exeter to Waterloo train. This train, loaded to 1? coaches and routed to Waterloo via Southampton, will need the combined 3100 hp of these two 'Cromptons' to keep the scheduled time of 3 hours 52 minutes, which includes 13 stops. *Roger Sivite*

Right, above: On 28 July 1991, Class 50 No 50033 *Glorious* speeds past the old goods shed at Chard Junction with the 11.05 train from Exeter to Waterloo. Chard Junction was the junction for the former GWR branch to Creech Junction on the GWR West of England main line, just to the east of Taunton. This branch line closed in 1962. Note the passing loop which was retained after closure of the station in 1966. *Roger Siviter*

Right, below: Although replaced by the Class 50s in 1980, Class 33s (as can also be seen elsewhere) were very often used as substitute power right up to the end of locomotive haulage on the route. On 26 March 1993, 'Crompton' No 33109 leaves the famous Devon carpet town of Axminster behind as it heads west with the 07.50 Basingstoke-Exeter train. Axminster was the junction for the branch line to Lyme Regis, which closed in 1965. At the rear of the train can be seen the banking and the abutments of the bridge which carried the branch line over the main line. *Geoff Gillham*

Opposite: Crewkerne station, which dates back to 1859, contrasts sharply with the modern BR type signal box. Running into the station on 15 August 1991 is the 14.22 Exeter to Waterloo train, hauled by Class 47/7 No 47709. Class 47/7 No 47701 to 47716 were all former ScotRail locomotives and were push-and-pull fitted for working the Glasgow to Edinburgh shuttle services. With electrification of the line between Scotland's two principal cities in the late 1980s, a lot of them were transferred to this route to replace the Class 50s, which by then had started to be withdrawn. *Roger Siviter*

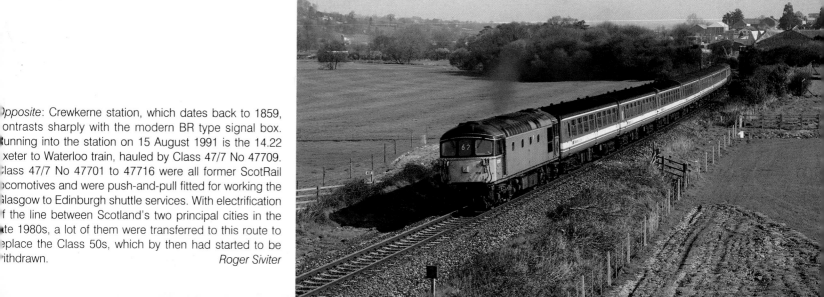

On a bright winter's day (19 February 1985) Class 50 No 50038 *Formidable* runs through the remains of Seaton Junction with the 11.10 Waterloo to Exeter train. There were originally four tracks through this once-busy station, the junction for the East Devon coastal resort of Seaton, the branch platform being situated off the right hand side of the picture. Both the branch line and Seato Junction station were closed in March 1966, but the main station building is commercial use.

Christina Sivit

After Seaton Junction, westbound trains face a steep 6 mile climb at 1 in 80 up to Honiton tunnel. The 31 August 1987 saw distinguished visitor to the line English Electric Class 40 No 40122 (D200) approaching the summit of Honiton bank with a Class 40 Appeal special train from Basingstoke to Exeter and return via Westbury. I should think that this is one of the few occasions when this famous class of diesel locomotives ran on this route.

Roger Siviter

Above: Looking very attractive in red and black Parcels Sector livery, Class 47/7 No 47712 *Lady Diana Spencer* runs smoothly up Honiton bank on 16 August 1991 with the 11.00 Waterloo to Exeter train. *Roger Siviter*

Opposite: On Sunday 28 July 1991, Class 50 No 50017 *Royal Oak* coasts dow the bank into Honiton station with the 08.15 Waterloo to Exeter train. As can b seen, the station is located on the hillside above the main part of this ea Devon market town. Honiton is also famous for lace-making. *Roger Sivit*

Right: As we approach Exeter, the line runs past Exmouth Junction where the old steam shed was located, and then runs through Blackboy tunnel where, on 31 August 1991, Class 47/7 No 47711 is seen emerging from its western portals with the 11.15 Waterloo to Exeter train. Above the fourth coach can be seen a concrete plate-layer's hut – a reminder of Southern Railway days. *Roger Siviter*

Opposite: Whimple, some 8 miles east of Honiton and home of the Whiteways Cider factory, is our next location as the 11.10 from Waterloo to Exeter, hauled by Class 50 No 50023 *Howe*, approaches the station on Sunday 27 March 1988. Apart from passing loops, the line is single from Yeovil to Pinhoe (3 miles from Exeter) and what looks like the up main line here was just used as an access siding. This siding was taken up in the summer of 1990. *Christina Siviter*

Right: Approaching Exeter Central station on Sunday 31 July 1983 is Class 47 No 47106 with the 11.10 Waterloo to Exeter train. In the early 1980s, Class 47 locomotives were not common on this route, this train being one of the few workings on which they would appear. Note the lovely old SR semaphore signals which by the date of our next picture at this location had long gone. On Tuesday 16 February 1988, Class 08 No 08941 runs towards Central station with a neat-looking train of cement tanks bound for the Blue Circle Cement depot situated to the side of the station. The semaphore signals in this area were replaced in April 1985, when Exeter St Davids power box came into operation.

Top: *Christina Siviter*. Bottom: *Roger Siviter*

Opposite: A half a mile before we reach Exeter Central station (172 miles from Waterloo) we pass through St James Park Halt, which is right by Exeter City's football ground – St James Park. On 28 April 1982, No 50035 *Ark Royal* passes through this small station with the 11.10 Waterloo to Exeter train. The adjacent allotments form an attractive backcloth.

Tom Heavyside

Above: Turning round from the previous scenes, we see the rear of a three-car DMU as it approaches Exeter Central station and passes the splendid LSWR signal box. The train is the 09.00 service from Exmouth and the date is 27 May 1984. Note the attractive five-arch road bridge, beyond which can be seen the roof of the concrete overbridge which straddles the up and down platforms and which also provides an extra entrance to the station (the North Road). The land on the right hand side is now a car park, but was originally carriage sidings and a coal depot.

Christina Siviter

Opposite: Some years later, on 16 August 1991, we see that the old LSW signal box is out of use, but it is still used as a tool store. It has now bee demolished. Approaching the camera is Class 33 No 33102 with the 07.4 from Basingstoke to Exeter.

Roger Sivite

This view of Exeter Central station was taken on 11 October 1987, by which time the centre roads had been taken out. Waiting to leave the up platform is Class 50 No 50009 *Conqueror* with the 14.20 from Exeter St Davids to Waterloo. On the right hand side is the cement depot and in the background on the left hand side can be seen the main Queen Street entrance to th[e] station. The original LSWR station on this site was known as Queen Street, th[e] SR Central station opening in 1933.

Roger Sivit[e]

On Saturday 30 July 1983, 'Crompton' No 33002 emerges from the shadows of Queen Street road bridge and enters Exeter Central station with the 13.35 Exeter St Davids to Waterloo, arriving in the capital at 17.09. At the rear of the train can be seen the steep bank which runs down to St Davids station, and on the right hand side the station signal box of LSWR design.   *Christina Siviter*

What a contrast to steam days, as the crew of Class 37 No 37258 exchange pleasantries as it glides smoothly up the 1 in 37 bank between St Davids and Central station with a train of concrete sleepers at 8am on Friday 3 May 1991.
Roger Siviter

Class 50 No 50008 *Thunderer* glows in the summer sunshine as it approaches Exeter Central on 30 July 1983 with the 11.40 from Exeter St Davids to Waterloo. A comparison with the previous picture shows that, over the intervening years, the factory unit in the centre of the picture has been demolished.

Christina Siviter

At midday on 28 April 1984, Class 33 No 33038 waits to leave Exeter St Davids platform 3 with the 12.20 service to Waterloo. Framing the scene is the famous signal gantry which, by the middle of the following year, would be a memory.

Roger Siviter

Although Exeter shed (83C) closed in 1964, it is still used for stabling locomotives and stock. On 28 April 1984, Class 08 shunting locomotive No 08840 pulls out of the old shed area on the western side of the station with the ECS for a Waterloo train. Looking on are a Peak Class 46 No 46028, Brush Class 47 No 47094 and an unidentified Peak Class 45, behind which is the nose of a Class 31 locomotive. The Peak Class were introduced in 1960 and the Class 08 shunters in 1953. Note the signal with route indicator and the old water crane.

Christina Sivite

On the same beautiful spring day as the last two pictures were taken, we see the rear of a Birmingham RC&W Co three-car suburban unit as it heads out of Exeter St Davids station with the 11.15 train to Barnstaple. It is just passing Exeter North signal box, which also controlled the goods yard, as well as the level crossing in the foreground. Note also the crossing man, very necessary in such a busy location.

Christina Siviter

Left: This magnificent GWR bracke signal at the northern end of St David station dominates the scene as Class 3 No 33062 accelerates past the ol goods shed with the 10.00 Exeter t Barnstaple service on Saturday 30 Ju 1983. This train will take one hour an three minutes for the 39 mile journey.

Christina Sivite

Opposite: In immaculate Railfreight liver Class 47 No 47339 pulls out of Exete Riverside yard on 16 February 1988 with lengthy train of empties bound for Meldo Ouarry, which is situated just to the sou of Oakhampton on the former SR line Plymouth. This line leaves the Barnstap line at Coleford Junction, some five mile west of Crediton.

Roger Sivite

opposite: Rare visitors to the Barnstaple line were the English Electric Class 20 locomotives. However, on 8 July 1984, a pair of Class 20s Nos 20184 and 20169 are seen approaching Cowley Bridge junction with a special train to Barnstaple from Plymouth, having worked to Devon's largest city earlier in the day from Bristol. At the time this picture was taken, semaphore signals still controlled the Exeter area but, as can be seen, colour light signalling was taking over and, as stated before, by the following year, with the opening of the new power box at St Davids station, semaphores would become redundant.

Christina Siviter

Above: On 5 September 1987, Class 31 No 31464 leaves the Barnstaple line and joins the former GWR West of England line at Cowley Bridge junction with the 10.13 Barnstaple to Exeter train. Just to the left of the locomotive is the site of the junction signal box, which was removed in 1985 with the Exeter re-signalling scheme. The ex-SR line to Barnstaple and Plymouth (via Oakhampton) was originally double track at the junction, but was singled in 1965.

Roger Siviter

This next picture, taken between Cowle and Half Moon Village on 26 Septembe 1987, clearly shows the trackbed of th removed line. The train is once again th 10.13 from Barnstaple to Exeter, only th time with Class 33 No 33023 in charge.

Christina Sivit

A busy scene at Crediton station, seven miles from Exeter, on a crisp winter's day – 18 February 1988. On the left hand side is the rear of a Derby Class 108 two-car DMU set No P957 leaving with the 10.48 Exeter to Barnstaple service, whilst departing from the up platform of this attractive former LSWR/SR station is the 10.10 Barnstaple to Exmouth train, which is formed by two sets of two-car units, the leading one being a Metropolitan-Cammell Class 101 set No 53330. These units were originally three-car sets and were introduced in 1958, as were the Class 108s.

Roger Siviter

Within thirty minutes of the previous picture, the scene was repeated only this time with Meldon Quarry trains. On the left hand side is Class 47 No 47624 heading light-engine to the quarry for another load of ballast, and approaching the camera is a pair of 'Cromptons', Nos 33026 and 33009, heading for Exeter with a loaded ballast train.

Roger Siviter

An unusual occurrence at Crediton on Saturday 5 September 1987, as English Electric Class 37 No 37175 and Brush Class 31 No 31464 double-head the 13.53 Barnstaple to Exeter train. Shortly after leaving Barnstaple, the Class 31 had failed and the Class 37 (from Exeter) had come to the rescue. The train is approaching the LSWR signal box with the signalman waiting to receive the single-line token. The line on the left hand side is to Oakhampton and Meldon Quarry. It leaves the Barnstaple line at Coleford Junction. Note the cross-over points for access to either line.

Christina Sivil

The next picture was taken at Eggesford, some 21 miles from Exeter, and shows the rear of the three-car DMU 18.45 Barnstaple to Exeter train as it leaves the station on 29 May 1984. The modern-looking signal box contrasts with the SR rail-built semaphore signal. *Christina Siviter*

As we have seen in the previous pictures, the Brush Class 31 diesels were no strangers to the Barnstaple line on summer Saturdays. On the afternoon of Saturday 26 September 1987, Class 31 No 31465 pulls away from its stop at Kings Nympton with the 15.48 from Exeter. This station was originally named South Molton Road after the market town some nine miles away! However, the name of accuracy, it was changed to its present title in 1948.

Christina Siviter

On 26 September 1987, we see the rear of the 15.00 Barnstaple to Exeter train as it pulls out of the former junction station. It is formed of two Class 142 'Skipper' DMUs Nos 142026 and 142018, both in chocolate and cream livery. These units were introduced in 1985, but only had a short stay in the West Country. On the left of the picture is the former SR-style signal box, in front of which are the lines that led to the loco shed (72E). *Roger Siviter*

Turning round from the last picture and on the same day, we see 'Crompton' No 33023 as it accelerates away from Barnstaple with the 13.53 service to Exeter. Note the mixture of semaphore signalling, a GWR-style bracket signal and, at the rear of the train, an upper quadrant rail-built SR signal. The Western Region took control of this former Southern line in 1964. The GWR always had a connection from its West of England main line to Barnstaple with a branch line from Taunton.

Roger Sivite

30390 3 O/C